HYDROPLANES

by
Hans Hetrick

Consultant:
Mark Wheeler
Vice President
American Power Boat Association (APBA)
Eastpointe, Michigan

CAPSTONE PRESS
a capstone imprint

Edge Books are published by Capstone Press,
151 Good Counsel Drive, P.O. Box 669, Mankato, Minnesota 56002.
www.capstonepub.com

Printed in the United States of America in North Mankato, Minnesota.
032010
005740CGF10

Books published by Capstone Press are manufactured with paper
containing at least 10 percent post-consumer waste.

Library of Congress Cataloging-in-Publication Data
Hetrick, Hans, 1973-
  Hydroplanes / by Hans Hetrick.
    p. cm.—(Edge books. Full throttle.)
  Includes bibliographical references and index.
  Summary: "Describes hydroplane boats, including their history, design, and the
races they participate in"—Provided by publisher.
  ISBN 978-1-4296-4753-3 (library binding)
  1. Hydroplanes—Juvenile literature. 2. Motorboat racing—Juvenile literature.
I. Title. II. Series.
  VM341.H486 2011
  623.82'04—dc22   2010000067

Editorial Credits
Carrie Braulick Sheely, editor; Ashlee Suker, designer; Laura Manthe,
    production specialist

Photo Credits
Alamy: Danita Delimont/Charles Sleicher, 26, Dennis MacDonald, 6, 16, fstop2/
Keith Pritchard, 14, Greg Gard, 21, Jim West, 18, 25; AP Images, 9, 13; DVIDS:
Courtesy Photo by H1 Unlimited/Chris Denslow, 28; Getty Images Inc.: Hulton
Archive/Keystone, 15; Newscom, 4, Newscom: Icon SMI/Jesse Beals, 23, Icon SMI/
John Pyle, 19, Icon SMI/Tom Suarez, 29, MCT/Detroit Free Press/Kathleen Galligan,
cover; Phil Kunz, 10; Shutterstock: Philipe Ancheta, 7

Artistic Effects
Dreamstime: In-finity, Michaelkovachev; iStockphoto: Michael Irwin, Russell Tate;
Shutterstock: Els Jooren, Fedorov Oleksiy, javarman, jgl247, Marilyn Volan, Pocike

Table of Contents

SPEEDING TO VICTORY

Steve David and Dave Villwock battled for the win. Three laps remained in the 2009 Chevrolet Cup hydroplane race in Seattle, Washington. Trailing Villwock, David tried to close in on his opponent. But then a wave knocked David's U-1 *Oh Boy! Oberto* hydroplane off balance. The front of the boat swept into the air. David came close to a **blowover**. Luckily, he managed to keep the U-1 under control. But while David was making the save, Villwock shot even farther ahead. Villwock sped off to victory in his bright orange U-16 *Ellstrom Elam Plus.*

For the first two laps, Steve David (left) and Dave Villwock (right) were in a head-to-head battle.

David and Villwock, along with several other drivers, race in the H1 Unlimited hydroplane series. The hydroplanes in this series are the world's fastest boats on **closed courses**. The boats can reach speeds of more than 200 miles (322 kilometers) per hour.

closed course—a race course that circles back to the starting line

blowover—a hydroplane accident in which the boat flips over backward

fast fact: Dave Villwock has won the National High Point Championship in the Unlimited series nine times.

A hydroplane looks like a giant lobster. Two **sponsons** reach out like big claws in front of the boat's body. The driver sits between the sponsons. A huge engine towers behind the driver in the middle of the boat.

A hydroplane is part boat and part airplane. Like other boats, it floats on the water. But as it speeds up, air sweeps under the boat's **hull**. The hydroplane then rises above the water. At high speeds, only three parts touch the water—the two sponsons and the propeller at the back. The sponsons skip back and forth over the waves, balancing the hydroplane. The propeller stays in the water and pushes the boat forward.

The sponsons constantly skip over the water. They may rise into the air at high speeds.

A hydroplane propeller creates one of the most remarkable sights in boat racing—the rooster tail. A rooster tail is a fountain of water that shoots high into the air behind the boat. Rooster tails are often three times as long as the boats themselves. Race announcers even use rooster tails to measure the length of leads in hydroplane races. An announcer might say, "Coming out of the north turn, U-16 has a two-rooster-tail lead."

sponson—a rounded part on each side of a hydroplane that keeps the boat steady

hull—the frame or body of a boat

2

HYDROPLANE HISTORY

Imagine a flat rock skipping over the water. It travels much farther and faster than a rock thrown into the water. Hydroplanes work on the same basic idea as a skipping rock.

In the 1870s, boat designers knew a boat could go faster on top of the water than through it. But the designers had no way of propelling a boat fast enough to test the idea. In the 1890s, more powerful engines finally gave boat builders the speed they needed to go airborne.

THE STEPPED HULL

The first hydroplanes looked like any other wooden boats traveling on the water. But beneath the water, the boat hulls had a step built into them. This type of hull was called a stepped hull. When the boat went fast enough, it used the step like a ramp. The boat made small jumps out of the water over and over again. In 1907, a single-step hydroplane reached almost 30 miles (48 km) per hour. When these hydroplanes raced by, drivers of other boats were stunned. Some said they felt as though they were "left standing as if we were at anchor."

Gar Wood

The stepped-hull boat design helped make Gar Wood a boat racing legend. In 1917, Wood and Christopher Smith built *Miss Detroit III*. It was the first boat to use an aircraft engine that was modified for use in a boat. The boat went on to win the famous Gold Cup race that year.

In the early 1900s, the Harmsworth races were considered some of the world's most important boat races. The winner of the race each year took home the prized Harmsworth Trophy. From 1920 to 1933, Wood blew away the competition with his *Miss America* boats. In 1990, Gar Wood was inducted into the Motorsports Hall of Fame of America.

Fast Fact: In 1916, the stepped-hull hydroplane *Miss Minneapolis* set a new boat world speed record. It averaged 55.8 miles (89.8 km) per hour for 5 miles (8 km).

THREE-POINT HYDROPLANES

Stepped-hull boats ruled boat racing until 1936. That year, the Ventnor Boat Works company of New Jersey came out with a new hydroplane design. Ventnor's hydroplanes were much wider than the stepped-hull designs. The new boats also had two large sponsons. The hydroplanes ran on three points—the two sponsons and the back of the boat, or stern. They became known as three-point hydroplanes.

Ventnor created the G-13 boat in 1938. Now restored to its original condition, the boat travels to boating events around the United States.

The sponsons were the key to the boats' better performance. At high speeds, the sponsons guided the rush of air under the boat. The air lifted the front of the boat, or bow, off the water. With less of the boat in the water, **drag** was reduced. Early three-point hydroplanes reached top speeds of around 60 miles (97 km) per hour.

drag—the force created when air or water strikes a moving object, slowing it down

From Water Skis to Hydroplanes

The three-point hydroplane design might have never happened without the Chinese military. In the 1930s, Ventor Boat Works owners agreed to build several boats for the Chinese military. The boats were required to meet one strict rule. They needed to reach speeds of up to 60 miles (97 km) per hour with 500 pounds (227 kilograms) in the bow. To keep the boats balanced, Ventnor designers turned to the water skis that they manufactured. They attached a water ski to each side of a boat. The skis helped keep the boat steady. Eventually, Ventnor turned the water skis into sponsons, creating their three-point hydroplane.

While the three-point design lifted the bow, the stern still dragged through the water. In 1945, Tommy Hill built one of the first boats to lift the stern out of the water. Hill's boat, the *Ly-Bee*, had a flat area at the front. The flat surface allowed air to push up against the boat's entire bottom. The air created enough force to lift the stern.

With the stern in the air, the propeller replaced it as the third point of contact. Hill's boat became known as a prop rider. The new design meant hydroplanes could finally skip over the water like a flat rock.

Ted Jones soon used Hill's prop-rider design on an Unlimited-class hydroplane. Jones' new prop rider, *Slo-Mo-Shun IV*, immediately started setting records. *Slo-Mo-Shun IV* shattered the straightaway world speed record in 1950. It averaged 160.3 miles (257.9 km) per hour. *Slo-Mo-Shun IV* also won the Gold Cup race in Detroit, Michigan, that year. Just two years later, *Slo-Mo-Shun IV* broke its own record. This time, it averaged 178.4 miles (287.1 km) per hour. The successful hydroplane continued racing in the Unlimited class until 1956. That year, a crash at the Gold Cup caused major damage to the boat.

In 1952, Stanley Dollar won the Gold Cup race in Slo-Mo-Shun IV.

Fast Fact: The *Ly-Bee's* propeller was the first to produce a rooster tail.

The prop rider marked the last major change in hydroplane design. But there were plenty of smaller changes to come. The most noticeable change was the **cockpit** location. Drivers of boats like *Slo-Mo-Shun IV* sat in a cockpit behind the engine. In the early 1960s, hydroplane designers experimented with engines mounted behind the drivers. In 1966, Ron Jones built one of the first successful rear-engine hydroplanes. Rear-mounted engines greatly improved visibility for drivers. They also made the boats more **aerodynamic**.

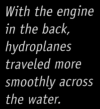

With the engine in the back, hydroplanes traveled more smoothly across the water.

Most other recent design changes have focused on safety. In 1986, designers started using fully enclosed cockpits. The covers, or canopies, were from military fighter jets. Made of strong plastic sheets, these canopies kept drivers safer in blowovers.

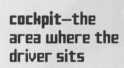

cockpit—the area where the driver sits

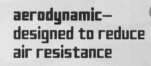

aerodynamic—designed to reduce air resistance

Fast Fact: In 1978, Ken Warby and the hydroplane *Spirit of Australia* set the current boat world speed record. His record stands at 317.6 miles (511.1 km) per hour.

15

3

THE STRUCTURE OF SPEED

Building a hydroplane for the H1 Unlimited class is no easy task. These top-notch hydroplanes take months or years to build. Boats need the perfect balance of power and control.

Designers follow general rules set up by H1 Unlimited. For example, boats have minimum weight rules and engine rules. But beyond these rules, each hydroplane is different. Designers must pay close attention to sponson shape and other details. One small part could mean the difference between a win and a loss.

Drivers must use the power of their boats wisely. Going too fast can cause a boat to flip.

HULL AND SPONSONS

Unlimited hydroplane hulls and sponsons are built with high-tech materials like **carbon fiber**, aluminum, and Kevlar. These materials are lightweight yet very strong. Hulls must be strong to withstand constant high-speed smacks of water.

Hull and sponson materials are also very easy to work with. Crews can make small repairs between races.

carbon fiber—a material made of strong, thin fibers held together by plastic

Fast Fact: Today's hydroplanes use a pickle-fork sponson design. This design has an empty space between the two sponsons.

ENGINES

Most hydroplanes in the Unlimited series use the T-55 Lycoming engine. The T-55 was originally designed for the Chinook, a large U.S. Army cargo helicopter. The gigantic engine burns through 4.1 gallons (15.5 liters) of fuel in a minute and produces about 2,650 horsepower.

The U-3 hydroplane is powered by a V-12 Allison engine. These engines were used by most hydroplanes from the 1950s through the 1980s. They were originally used in military airplanes in World War II (1939–1945). Even though the U-3 has an older engine, it has no problem keeping up with the competition.

Unlimited-series teams have extra engines at races in case one breaks and needs to be replaced.

Salt-Water Solutions

When hydroplanes race in salt water, they use a snorkel. Salt water can ruin a hydroplane engine. A snorkel extends the engine cover, or cowling, forward over the cockpit. With the snorkel, water spray can't get into the engine and cause a breakdown.

snorkel

PROPELLER

The right propeller, or "prop," can make a huge difference in hydroplane performance. Unlimited racing teams have a number of propellers available on race day. Some propellers have thicker blades than others. The angle of the propeller blades also varies.

Crews choose propellers based on the weather conditions and the racetrack size and shape. On a short course, a propeller might be chosen to help the hydroplane **accelerate**. On a long course, a crew might choose a propeller that reduces acceleration but increases top speed.

accelerate—to gain speed

Fast Fact: One propeller for the *Oh Boy! Oberto* hydroplane is worth about $15,000.

RUDDER AND SKID FIN

The rudder and the skid fin slice through the water underneath the hydroplane. The rudder is a wedge-shaped blade that turns the boat. It is usually mounted on the right side at the back of the boat.

The skid fin is located at the back of the left sponson. It grabs the water and balances the boat in high-speed turns. The skid fin can kick up a second rooster tail 30 feet (9 meters) in the air.

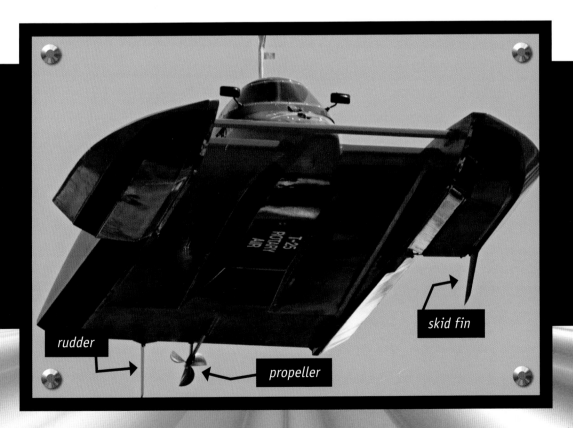

rudder

propeller

skid fin

CANARD

Flying over the water at high speeds is risky. Hydroplanes can soar into the air and blow over at any moment. The canard stretches between the sponsons at the boat's front. Drivers use it to control the boat's **lift**. They angle the canard down to reduce lift and prevent blowovers. They angle the canard up to increase lift when the boat is catching too much water.

COCKPIT

Before the late 1980s, hydroplane accidents were much more dangerous. The cockpits had few safety features. But modern cockpits have a number of safety features. An escape hatch is built into the cockpit's bottom. Drivers can exit through the hatch if the boat lands upside down after a blowover. A **roll cage** surrounds the driver. A strong safety harness straps the driver into the seat.

All cockpits are also equipped with an onboard air supply in case the cockpit fills with water. The air flows through a hose that connects to the driver's helmet.

lift—the distance to which something rises

roll cage—strong tubing that surrounds and protects a driver during crashes

Length:	about 30 feet (9 meters)
Width:	about 14 feet (4 meters)
Weight:	6,200 to 7,000 pounds (2,812 to 3,175 kilograms)
Hull material:	aluminum, carbon fiber, Kevlar, fiberglass
Top speed:	about 220 miles per hour (354 kilometers)
Engine:	usually a T-55 Lycoming turbine
Horsepower:	about 2,650
Fuel type:	jet fuel
Fuel capacity:	60 gallons (227 liters)
Fuel consumption:	4.1 gallons (15.5 liters) per minute
Propeller:	three-blade stainless steel

Each driver wears a helmet and a full racing suit for protection during crashes.

In a 2006 Unlimited race, J. Michael Kelly bumped into another driver's hydroplane. Kelly lost control of his U-13 hydroplane, and the boat flipped into the air. Then disaster nearly struck. Kelly's boat came within inches of crashing into Steve David's cockpit.

After the race, David breathed a huge sigh of relief. According to a local TV station, David said, "I knew it was pretty close. Nothing you could do. It just happens too fast. We had no place to go … You just ride through and hope." Kelly was also fortunate. He escaped the accident with minor injuries.

Each Unlimited hydroplane race is full of exciting—and sometimes scary—moments. Since 1946, six sites have held most of the Unlimited races. They include Detroit, Michigan; Madison, Indiana; and Evansville, Indiana. Also included are San Diego, California; Seattle, Washington; and the Tri-Cities region of Washington. Detroit is home to the Gold Cup, the longest-running Unlimited race. Seattle is home to the popular Seafair race. Nearly all of the Unlimited teams have their home port in or nearby these six race sites.

Three Unlimited hydroplanes fight for the win during the 2005 Gold Cup on the Detroit River.

Fast Fact: The citizens of Madison, Indiana, own the *Oh Boy! Oberto* Unlimited hydroplane. It is the only hydroplane owned by citizens of a city.

Unlimited hydroplane races begin with a **flying start**. The oval courses are between 2 and 2.5 miles (3.2 and 4 km) long. The courses are marked off by buoys. Drivers must stay to the outside of the buoys as they race.

Seattle's Seafair Festival hydroplane races are held on Lake Washington each year.

flying start—crossing the starting line at top speeds instead of from a stop

As they compete in races, H1 drivers earn points toward the National High Point Championship. Each race has three preliminary heats and one final heat. The preliminary heats are three laps, and the final heat is five laps.

The five drivers with the most points after the preliminary heats advance to the final heat. The winner of the final heat wins the whole event, regardless of the point total.

Drivers also win points based on their final-heat performance. The number of points drivers earn decreases with their placings. Drivers earn 40 points for first place. Fifth-place earns 13 points.

At the end of the season, the driver with the most final-heat points is crowned the high-point champion. The champion driver wins prize money. This driver also has the honor of placing the U-1 title on his boat for the next season.

A STEP BEYOND THE BORDERS

The sport of hydroplane racing gets bigger every year. The last race of the 2009 season took H1 Unlimited hydroplanes across the world. The race was held in the Middle Eastern country of Qatar. As the Unlimited series attracts more fans, the fearless drivers will be ready for the world stage.

Steve David races Oh-Boy! Oberto in Qatar in 2009.

Fast Fact: Although the high-point champion driver races the U-1 boat, the other "U" boat numbers don't indicate rankings.

Drag Boat Racing

Hydroplanes don't just race around oval courses and turn left. They also compete in drag races. Boat drag races are similar to car drag races. Two boats race in a straight line over a set distance. Hydroplane races are usually .25-mile (0.4-km) long. The race starts when the light turns green. To make sure the boats begin in a straight line, a rope pulls them before the start.

Most often, drag-boat racers compete in elimination rounds. Two hydroplanes are pitted against each other. The winner of each round advances to the next round. Drivers face off against each other until one is crowned champion.

GLOSSARY

accelerate (ak-SEL-uh-rayt)—to gain speed

aerodynamic (air-oh-dye-NA-mik)—designed to reduce air resistance

blowover (BLOH-oh-vur)—a hydroplane accident in which the boat lifts into the air and flips over backward

bow (BOU)—the front of a boat

carbon fiber (KAHR-buhn FYE-bur)—a material made of strong, thin fibers held together by plastic

closed course (KLOHZD KORSS)—a race course that circles back to the starting line

cockpit (KOK-pit)—the area in a hydroplane where the driver sits

drag (DRAG)—the force created when air or water strikes a moving object, slowing it down

flying start (FLYE-ing START)—a race start in which a vehicle crosses the starting line at full speed instead of from a stop

home port (HOME PORT)—the home base and garage of a hydroplane where it can be repaired and tested

hull (HUHL)—the frame or body of a boat

lift (LIFT)—the distance to which something rises

roll cage (ROHL KAYJ)—a structure of strong tubing that surrounds the driver for protection during crashes

rooster tail (ROO-stur TAYL)—a high stream of water kicked up behind a hydroplane by the propeller or the skid fin

sponson (SPAWN-sen)—a part on the side of a hydroplane that helps keep the boat steady

READ MORE

Hofer, Charles. *Speedboats*. World's Fastest Machines. New York: PowerKids Press, 2008.

Schuh, Mari. *Full Speed Ahead: The Science of Going Fast*. Shockwave Science. New York: Children's Press, 2008.

Tieck, Sarah. *Speedboats*. Amazing Vehicles. Edina, Minn.: ABDO Pub. Co., 2010.

INTERNET SITES

FactHound offers a safe, fun way to find Internet sites related to this book. All of the sites on FactHound have been researched by our staff.

Here's all you do:

Visit *www.facthound.com*

FactHound will fetch the best sites for you!

Index